The Story of Your Ear

by Dr. Alvin Silverstein and Virginia B. Silverstein

illustrated by Susan Gaber

Coward, McCann & Geoghegan · New York

Text copyright © 1981 by Alvin and Virginia
B. Silverstein
Illustrations copyright © 1981 by Susan Gaber
Library of Congress Cataloging in Publication Data
Silverstein, Alvin.
  The story of your ear.
  Includes index.
  SUMMARY: Describes the structure of the ear,
what sound is and how the ear receives it, the ear's
role in maintaining balance, and how the ear can be
damaged.
  1. Ear—Juvenile literature.   2. Hearing—
Juvenile literature. [1. Ear.   2. Hearing]
I. Silverstein, Virginia B., joint author.
II. Gaber, Susan. III. Title.
QP462.2.S58   612'.85   80-17052
ISBN 0-698-30704-6

Printed in the United States of America
Second Impression

Contents

A World of Sounds

Shh. Listen! Close your eyes and concentrate. What do you hear?

Perhaps you are reading in your room. A moment ago you might have said that all was quiet. But now that you are *listening,* you are suddenly aware of a world of sounds: the hum of an electric clock, the rush of water running through the pipes, people's voices in another room, the honking of cars in the street outside or the rumble of trucks on a distant highway, a dog barking somewhere, a wisp of music from a radio . . .

Maybe you're trying to read in a crowded lunchroom. Before you *listened,* you were aware only of a confused blur of background noise. But now you can pick out bits of conversations, the clanking of dishes, and the shuffling and bumping of people moving around, carrying trays, getting up and sitting down.

Imagine what your life would be like if you couldn't hear anything—if the whole world around you were silent. No music. No wind rustling the leaves. No sound of water gurgling out of the faucet. No alarm clock to wake you up in the morning. No sound of speech. Imagine what it would be like if you couldn't talk with people and hear their answers!

Sounds bring a world of interesting and important information. We hear these sounds with a pair of special sense organs, the ears.

1 A Look at the Ear

The ears you see on the sides of people's heads are really only a part of the organ of hearing—and not the most important part, in fact. The outer ear—the part you can see—is also called the *pinna.* It leads inward through a curving tube to a bony chamber called the middle ear. Still farther inside, nestled within another hollow in the bones of the skull, is the third part, the inner ear.

Our ears aren't very impressive, compared with the ears of some other members of the animal kingdom. Each outer ear, or *pinna,* of an African elephant may measure as much as three feet across. A little North African fox called the fennec has wide ears that are three inches tall. That's not elephant-sized, but each of the fennec's pinnae is larger than its whole face! A rabbit's ears are long and narrow. They may be carried folded flat against the rabbit's back or held straight up above its head.

The ears of the elephant, fennec and rabbit are real sound funnels.

Horses and dogs can use their outer ears more efficiently than we can.

The outer ear works as a sound-gathering funnel. Many animals have special muscles that can move their ears to make them more effective sound gatherers. Have you ever noticed a dog or horse pricking up its ears when it is alert? It can raise its ears, lower them, and turn them like a radar antenna, pointing them at an interesting sound. Humans have ear-moving muscles, too, but most of us can't use them. Even if you can wiggle your ears, you can't turn them toward sounds the way a dog or horse can.

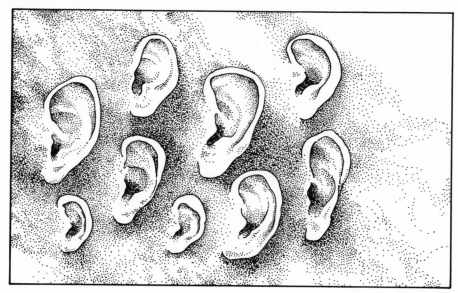

Pinnae

If you look at people's ears, you will notice many differences in shape. Some ears are long and narrow. Others are short and wide. Some people have large earlobes (the fleshy part at the bottom of the ear); others have hardly any earlobes at all. Some earlobes hang free; others are solidly attached to the skin of the face. The shape of the ears is hereditary: your ears probably look just like either your mother's or your father's. Looking at family pictures, you will see the same ear shapes popping up again and again, through the generations.

Even though people's ears may have somewhat different shapes, they all follow the same basic pattern. The human pinna is a rather flat structure, attached to the side of the head like a saucer sitting on a table. If you feel your ear, you will notice that it is fairly firm, but not hard. Its inner structure is not made of bone, but of a substance called cartilage. (The chewy "gristle" on the end of a chicken bone is cartilage.) The cartilage of the ear is rather elastic, so that if you bend your ear, it will snap back into place. The cartilage framework can be damaged by a hard blow to the ear, and when it heals, extra tissue grows over it. That is how the typical "cauliflower ear" of the boxer develops.

The curves and folds of the pinna lead into a slightly curved canal that is about an inch (or 2.5 centimeters) long. The curved shape of this ear canal (also called the *external acoustic* or *auditory meatus*) helps to protect the ear from things getting into it. A doctor pulls the pinna up and back to look into the ear. Pulling the pinna this way also makes it easier to apply ear drops.

The ear canal is lined with skin, which is very thick in the outer part and very thin in the inner part. There is not much feeling in the outer half of the ear canal, but the skin lining the inner half is very sensitive. If something touches it, this can be really painful.

Bristly hairs near the opening of the ear canal help to screen out dust particles and trap small insects that might wander into the ear. Further protection is provided by the sticky, yellowish earwax. This wax, which scientists call *cerumen,* is produced by a special kind of sweat glands *(ceruminous glands)* in the skin lining the canal. It helps to keep the ear canal smooth and moist, and it also traps any insects or small particles that get past the hairs guarding the entrance to the ear.

The canal leads from the outer ear to the *middle ear* chamber, which is like a cave hollowed out in the bones of the skull. Stretched across the entrance to the middle ear is a thin membrane, the *eardrum.*

Within the middle ear cavity are three tiny bones, forming a bridge between the eardrum and another membrane that covers the entrance to the inner ear.

The *inner ear* is another cavern hollowed out in the bones of the skull. It contains a number of tiny structures: the *cochlea,* which is coiled like a snail shell; two fluid-filled membranous bags called the *saccule* and the *utricle;* and three looping structures, something like the turns of a pretzel, called the *semicircular canals.*

Before we look more closely into the middle and inner ears and how their structures work, let's find out more about sound.

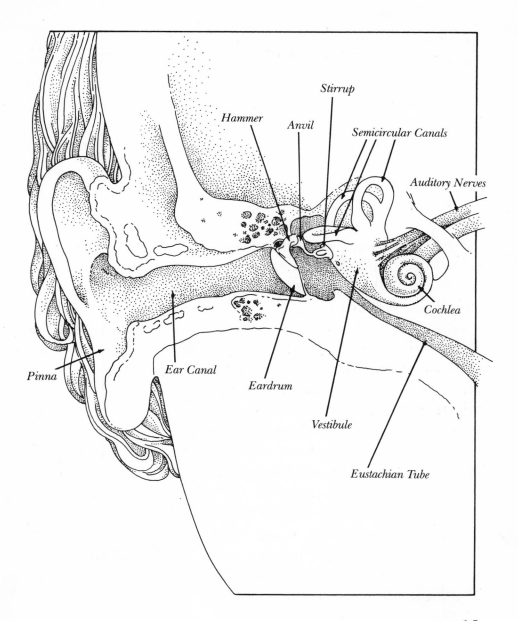

Hammer

Anvil

Stirrup

Semicircular Canals

Auditory Nerves

Cochlea

Pinna

Ear Canal

Eardrum

Vestibule

Eustachian Tube

13

2 What Is Sound?

If you have ever bounced up and down on your bed, you know that the mattress first gets flattened under the weight of your body, and then springs back into shape. If you could watch the coiled springs inside the mattress in slow motion, you would see that at first the coils closest to your body are pressed together. Then, as these coils are moving back to their normal spacing, the coils farther down are being compressed, and so on. It seems as though a wave of compression is passing down the spring, until it reaches the bottom. Then the wave of compression moves back up the spring until finally all the coils are back to their normal spacing.

A sound travels through the air in much the same way as a wave of compression travels along a coiled spring. It is carried along by the tiny, invisible gas molecules that make up the air around us. Sound is a form of energy that can make molecules move. But the molecules don't move very far. They just go until

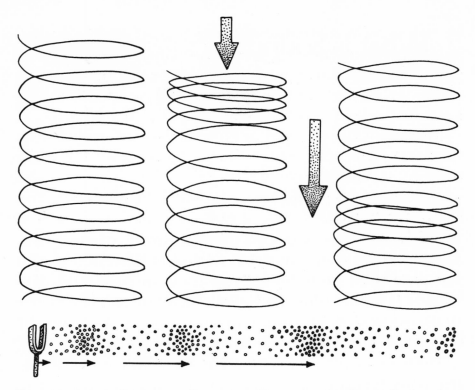

Energy can produce a moving wave of compression in a coiled spring (top) and in air molecules (bottom).

they bump into other molecules. These molecules bump into still other molecules, and so on. The waves of bumping molecules can carry the sound over long distances.

The energies involved in sound waves can be amazingly small. Scientists have calculated that a brass band of ten million instruments, playing as loud as it can, would be needed to generate just one horsepower of sound energy. Or, if sound energy could be changed into heat, one million people would have to talk for an hour and a half just to warm up a cup of tea.

Light is another form of energy that can travel long distances. But light travels faster than sound. During a thunderstorm, you can tell just about how far away the lightning is by counting the seconds between the lightning flash and the rumbling thunder. Each five seconds you count means about a mile of distance. Even though both the light of the lightning and the sound of the thunder started out at the same time, the light reaches you much sooner, for light can travel at a speed of about 186,000 miles per second (or about 300,000 kilometers per second), while sound travels at a speed of only 1,100 feet per second (or 330 meters per second).

There is another important difference between light and sound. Light can travel even through a vacuum. Traveling through air slows it down slightly, and traveling through a liquid medium like water, or through a solid like glass, slows it down even more. But sounds can't travel unless there are molecules to bump against each other. Have you ever seen a Western movie in which the Indian scout put his ear to the ground to hear the distant hoofbeats better? He was using the fact that sound travels faster through the solid ground than it does through the air.

The sounds you hear are not all alike. They may be high or low, loud or soft. The term *pitch* refers to how high or low a sound is. The pitch of a sound is determined by the frequency of the sound waves—how many waves are passing each second. (Each passing wave is referred to as a cycle.) The human ear can hear sounds from about 20 cycles per second (or cps) up to about 20,000 cps. (The smaller numbers correspond to the lower tones and the larger ones to the higher tones.)

There are sounds that we can't hear. When you hear a mouse squeak, you are hearing only part of the squeak. Mice also produce very high-pitched sounds, far above the 20,000 cps ceiling for human ears. The ears of mice can detect these sounds, and the mice can signal to each other with sounds that are not heard by us. Cats' ears can pick up these high-pitched sounds, too. They tune in on the mice's "conversations" and use the squeaks to help them find their prey. Other animals can also hear sounds that we can't. A dog whistle uses high-frequency sounds to call the dog without disturbing people.

Human ears are most sensitive to sounds with frequencies between 1,000 and 4,000 cycles per second. Oddly enough, that isn't the typical range for human speech. A man's voice produces sounds mainly around 100 cps, and the basic tone of a woman's voice is around 150 cps. But human speech also uses high-pitched hisses. Have you ever noticed that speech is often harder to understand over the telephone than it is in person? The telephone transmits the basic voice tones but not the high-pitched hisses, so speech doesn't sound quite the same as it does face to face.

The strings of a guitar are each tuned to produce a sound of a different pitch. The tighter (and therefore shorter) the string, the higher the tone. If you pluck a guitar string very gently and then pluck it hard, it will still produce a sound of the same pitch. But the sound will be much louder if you pluck it hard. If you watch the string closely, you will see that it is vibrating more forcefully, sweeping back and forth over a wider area and thus setting more molecules bumping into their neighbors. The loudness of a sound thus depends on how wide the vibrations are—what scientists call their *amplitude*.

The loudness of sounds is measured in a special scale called the decibel scale. It was named after Alexander Graham Bell, who invented the telephone. The decibel scale goes up very quickly, by multiplying rather than adding. A sound with a rating of 20 decibels (or db) is ten times as loud as a sound rated at 10 db. A 30 db sound is one hundred times as loud as a 10 db sound, 40 db one thousand times, and so on. Your ear can hear sounds over a wide range of loudness: the loudest

18

Type of Sound	Decibel Ratings	
Whisper	20 db	
Normal Conversation	60 db	
Heavy Traffic	80 db	
Amplified Music	140 db	
Jet Plane Taking Off	160 db	

sound you can hear is about a trillion times as loud as the softest sound you can detect.

On the decibel scale, a whisper has a loudness of about 20 db. A normal conversation rates about 60 db. Heavy traffic noise has a loudness about 80 db, a hundred times as loud as a conversation. A noise of 120 db is uncomfortable to hear, and 140 db may be painful. The typical amplified music at a discotheque blasts away as high as 140 db. A jet plane at takeoff rates 160 db.

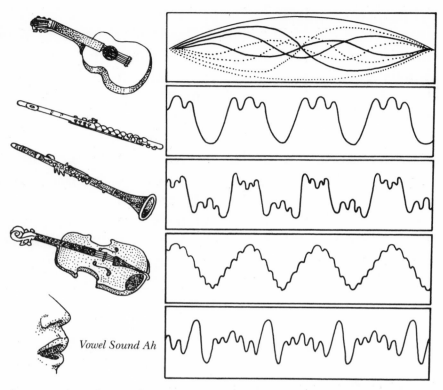

Vowel Sound Ah

At the top: A guitar string vibrates in a complex way. In addition to the fundamental vibration of its full length, it also vibrates in fractions of its length—halves, thirds, fourths, and so on. When all the waves of a complex vibration are summed up, they make a pattern such as those shown below for several musical instruments and the human voice. Different instruments playing the same note can thus produce quite different sounds.

Pitch and amplitude don't tell the whole story of sounds. If a piano, a guitar, and a saxophone each played in turn a note of exactly the same pitch and exactly the same loudness, you would still be able to tell the difference between them. For each instrument produces not only the basic sound frequency, but also overtones—sounds that are higher or lower than the basic frequency. The combination of the basic pitch and the overtones makes up the quality or *timbre* of a particular sound.

Our ears permit us to pick up sounds, to distinguish between high and low tones, loud and soft ones, and to sort them into meaningful patterns. Let's find out more about how they work.

3 Inside the Ear: The Middle Ear

Sound vibrations, traveling through the air, are funneled down the outer ear canal and press on the eardrum, a membrane of very thin skin stretched across the entrance to the middle ear. Like the head of a drum, the eardrum can be set vibrating when a force is applied to it. When you tap a drum with a drumstick, you are applying a rather large force, whereas the amount of energy contained in sound waves is very tiny. But the human eardrum is amazingly sensitive. It can pick up the minute pressure changes in the air produced by sound waves. When it vibrates, its movements are astonishingly small. A sound will set your eardrums moving in and out by as little as a billionth of a centimeter (0.000000001 cm or 0.0000000004 inch). That is as small as the diameter of a hydrogen atom, the smallest atom of all the chemical elements. Loud sounds produce larger movements of the eardrum. If an insect manages to get past the defenses in the ear canal and walks across the eardrum, its tiny feet can move the membrane enough to produce a deafening noise. It sounds like an elephant clumping around on a tin roof!

How can such small vibrations be transmitted into the inner chambers of the ear? This is accomplished in an ingenious way. Resting on the inside of the eardrum is a tiny bone, the other end of which is tied by tough ligaments to a second tiny bone. The end of that bone is tied to still a third bone, which completes the bridge across the middle ear cavity to the entrance to the inner

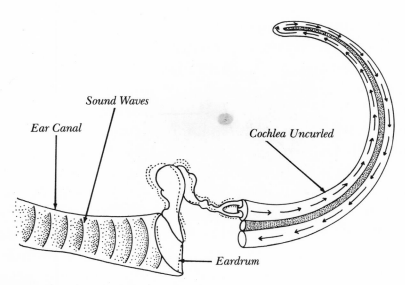

Vibrations passing through eardrum, ossicles and cochlea.

ear. These three little bones are called the *ossicles,* which means "little bones."

The scientist who first described the bones of the middle ear thought that their shapes looked like those of some familiar objects, and so he named these three bones the *hammer,* the *anvil,* and the *stirrup.* In more formal terminology they are called, respectively, the *malleus,* the *incus,* and the *stapes.* The handle of the hammer (malleus) rests on the eardrum, and its head seems to strike the anvil (incus). The anvil, in turn, presses against the top of the stirrup (stapes), and the "foot" of the stirrup rests against the *oval window,* the membrane that covers the entrance to the inner ear.

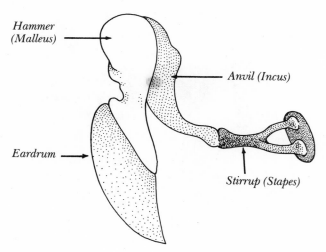

Eardrum and ossicles

Vibrations of the eardrum set the hammer jiggling. It jiggles against the anvil and sets it vibrating, too. The vibrations are transmitted to the stirrup, and finally to the oval window. Because of the shapes of the little bones, the forces from the eardrum are transmitted from a fairly wide area to a very small one, at the footplate of the stirrup on the oval window. This decrease in area multiplies the force being applied by about twenty-two times. An example of this force-multiplying principle is a woman's spike-heeled shoes. A hundred-pound woman walking barefoot would have her weight distributed over about a quarter of a square foot, and so would be applying a pressure of about 400 pounds per square foot on the floor. But in spike heels, her entire weight would be concentrated on a much smaller area. Every time she took a step, she would be applying a pressure of about 10,000 pounds per square foot—enough to make a dent in a linoleum floor.

When exceedingly loud noises set the eardrum vibrating very strongly, special muscles in the middle ear tighten the ligaments that hold the tiny ossicles together. Their action helps to cut down the vibrations of the bones and protects the inner ear from heavy blows that might damage it.

You have probably seen a number of chicken bones and bones of other animals used for meat. You may have seen whole skeletons of humans and animals—

even dinosaurs—in a museum. From these everyday experiences, you probably think of bones as being rather large. It's hard to realize just how small the hammer, anvil, and stirrup actually are. To give you an idea: the middle ear cavity in which they lie is so small that it would be filled by just five drops of liquid from a medicine dropper.

The middle ear is filled with air, which is normally at the same pressure as the air outside. The pressures are

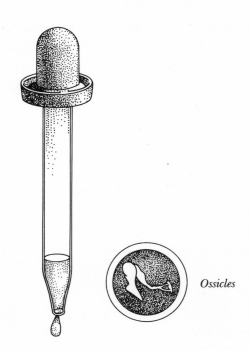

Ossicles

kept equal by a tube called the *eustachian tube,* which connects the middle ear to the pharynx, the air passage that comes down from the nose to the throat. Most of the time the eustachian tube is closed, but it opens automatically whenever you swallow, yawn, or move your jaw in chewing. When you go up or down very rapidly in an elevator or an airplane, the pressure outside changes too quickly for the middle ear to keep up, and the eustachian tubes may be squeezed shut. Then your ears may pop or squeak painfully, and you may even become temporarily deaf. The unpleasant feeling can usually be relieved by swallowing or yawning, which helps to open the eustachian tubes. On a plane, the flight attendant usually recommends chewing gum.

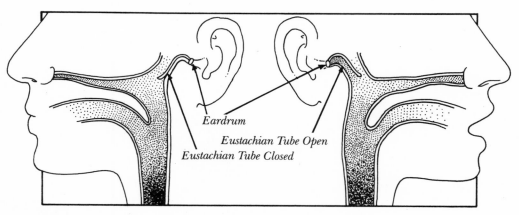

Eardrum

Eustachian Tube Open

Eustachian Tube Closed

The eustachian tube in closed and open positions

A head cold, which causes the eustachian tubes to become blocked by swollen membranes and mucus, can lead to ear trouble. Some of the air trapped in the middle ear cavities dissolves in the tissues, creating a slight vacuum in the chamber. The pressure difference can't be equalized properly because the connecting tubes are blocked. So the eardrums bulge inward, making them less able to vibrate and producing a tight, stuffed feeling in the ears. Blowing your nose hard with your mouth closed can also force germ-laden air into the middle ear and may cause an ear infection. Such infections can be dangerous for two reasons. They cause a loss of hearing (which will usually clear up if the infection is treated promptly), and they may spread into the neighboring mastoid bone, which leads to the brain.

4 Inside the Ear: The Inner Ear

In ancient Crete, so the story goes, a monster called the Minotaur lived in the center of the Labyrinth. The Labyrinth was a huge maze of winding, branching tunnels and passageways, so confusing that only a few people knew how to find their way through it. The chamber of the inner ear, the *labyrinth,* was named after this ancient maze. No monster lurks inside the labyrinth of the ear, but its passageways certainly do form a confusing-looking maze.

The *oval window,* the entrance to the inner ear, leads into a region called the *vestibule.* This is a sort of "front hallway," in which two membranous bags, the saccule and utricle, are found. The vestibule opens into the cochlea, which is shaped like a snail shell, and the three semicircular canals. The passages of the "maze" cut through the bones of the skull and are lined with membranes, so there is both a bony labyrinth and a smaller, membrane labyrinth inside it. Unlike the middle ear cavity, the labyrinth is filled with fluid.

You may be surprised to learn that only one of the structures in the inner ear is concerned with hearing. This is the cochlea. The saccule, utricle, and semicircular canals all have a different job in the body's sense system: they are involved in the sense of balance. This important sense will be discussed in a later chapter.

The oval window leads from the middle ear into the inner ear. There is another window in the labyrinth, called the *round window*. It is also covered by a membrane, but it doesn't lead anywhere. What does it do? It acts as a sort of safety valve.

In a gas like air, there is a lot of space between molecules. If you put pressure on a gas in a closed space, the molecules simply move closer together, and the volume they occupy gets smaller. In other words, a gas can be compressed. So when the eardrum vibrates and moves inward into the chamber of the middle ear, it compresses the air inside the chamber. Then, when the eardrum moves outward, the air expands again to fill up the larger volume. No "safety valve" is needed for the middle ear. But the inner ear is not filled with air; it is filled with fluid. Liquids can't be compressed. If you put pressure on them, they will flow, but they will still take up the same volume.

Now, imagine what would happen if there were only one membrane-covered opening into the labyrinth of

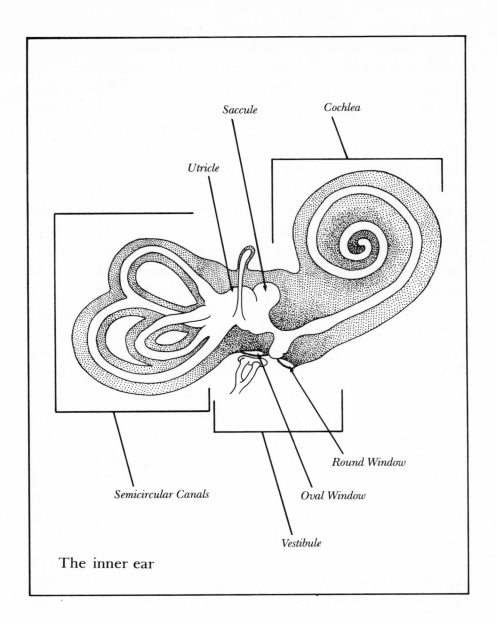

Saccule

Cochlea

Utricle

Round Window

Semicircular Canals

Oval Window

Vestibule

The inner ear

the inner ear. A sound strikes the eardrum. It vibrates, and its vibrations are transmitted along the three tiny ear bones to the membrane of the oval window. The membrane vibrates and presses in on the fluid in the labyrinth. A wave of pressure shoots out into the fluid and "loops the loop" around the coils of the cochlea. Then it flows . . . where? If there were no other opening, the wave would batter against the walls of the inner ear and give you a terrible headache. But the round window solves the problem. Whenever the oval window presses inward, the membrane of the round window promptly bulges outward, by exactly the same amount. When the oval window vibrates outward, the round window moves inward. In this way, the moving fluid has a place to go.

The cochlea coils for about two and a half turns. Inside, this coiling canal is divided by two membranes into three channels that run the length of the spiral. There is an upper channel, a lower channel, and a middle channel that looks something like a wedge-shaped worm winding its way through a snail shell. The floor of the central channel is formed by a membrane called the *basilar membrane*. More than twenty thousand stiff, hairlike fibers are laid out crosswise along this membrane. These basilar fibers gradually increase in size, from about four hundreths of a millimeter long at the base of the cochlea to about half a millimeter at the tip of the coil. They can vibrate,

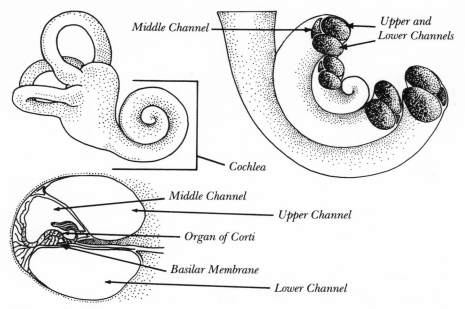

Middle Channel

Upper and Lower Channels

Cochlea

Middle Channel

Upper Channel

Organ of Corti

Basilar Membrane

Lower Channel

The cochlea in detail

like the reeds of a harmonica or the strings of a harp. Each fiber vibrates at its own frequency. As you might expect, the shorter fibers vibrate at higher frequencies, and the longer ones vibrate at lower frequencies.

Resting upon the basilar membrane is a structure called the *organ of Corti.* This is a ridge made up of two kinds of cells. One kind is the supporting cells. They provide a support for the other type, the hair cells. The organ of Corti has about fifteen thousand hair cells. Each one contains a tiny, hairlike structure that sticks

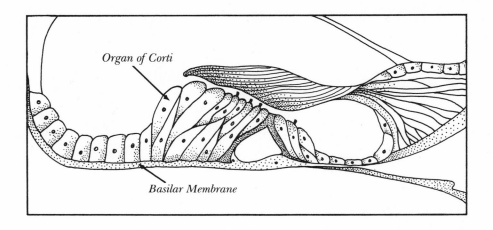

out into the fluid-filled channel. The tips of the hairs are covered with a jellylike substance.

Now we've met the most important characters in the story of your ear. Let's find out more about what they do.

5 How You Hear

"Let's hear an A," says the conductor. And from a hundred voices, the tone of an A rings out. Sound waves travel through the air, as molecules bump into each other and bounce back, while a series of new bumps and bounces carries on. In a fraction of a second, the sound waves reach your ear canal. Down the funnel they go and set your eardrum vibrating. The vibrations of the eardrum are picked up and amplified by the jiggling bones of the middle ear. They travel along the hammer, anvil, and stirrup to the oval window and set that vibrating, too.

As the oval window vibrates, pressure waves are set up in the fluid of the inner ear. Waves race up and down the coils of the cochlea. The basilar membrane is quite elastic. The pressure causes it to bulge out, and then it bounces back. A wave travels up the basilar membrane, until it reaches the fibers that can vibrate at just the right frequency to match it. Now the vibrating fibers are like bucking broncos, on which the cells of the organ of Corti are riding. The vibrations of the basilar fibers cause the hair cells that rest on them to bend, first in one direction and then in the other.

The structures of the ear have done their work. But you haven't *heard* anything yet. There is another chapter to the story.

A tiny, threadlike nerve fiber runs from each hair cell in the organ of Corti. When a vibration causes a hair cell to bend back and forth, a message is sent along the nerve fiber. The thousands of tiny nerve fibers from the hair cells are gathered into a rope of fibers called the *cochlear nerve*. Messages from the cochlear nerve are carried to the brain. There they are relayed to various parts of the brain and finally reach the cerebral cortex, its thinking part.

A special hearing center in the cortex sorts out the information carried by the nerve cells. There are different spots in this center that correspond exactly to each point on the basilar membrane. In this way, the brain can determine just what the pitch of the sound was, according to which hair cells were excited. Messages from the nerves also carry information on how loud the sounds were. Loud sounds make the nerve cells fire faster. They also excite more hair cells, so that a big noise produces a stronger nerve message. In addition, some of the hair cells act as special watchdogs. They are very hard to excite, and their nerve

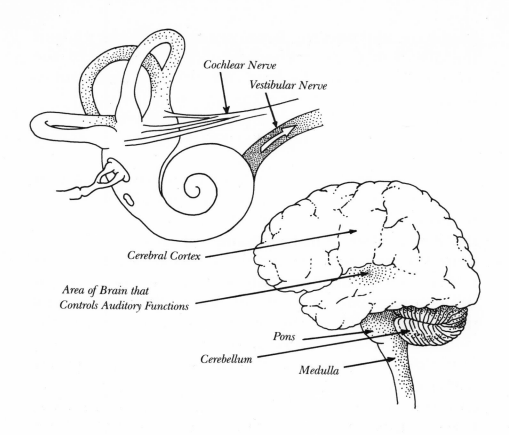

Cochlear Nerve

Vestibular Nerve

Cerebral Cortex

Area of Brain that
Controls Auditory Functions

Pons

Cerebellum

Medulla

fibers never fire at all unless a sound is particularly loud. So a message from these particular hair cells is a signal of a very loud noise.

The brain puts all this information together to form a pattern. And at last, you *hear*.

6 Hearing What You Want to Hear

Don't you wish sometimes that you could close your ears? When a pneumatic drill is going rat-a-tat in the street outside, or a jet plane is roaring overhead, or someone is scolding you, it would be wonderful to just shut your ear canals and shut out the unwanted sound.

Some animals *can* close their ears. When a seal or sea otter dives into the sea, special muscles clamp together and close its ears to keep water from getting into them. (A whale doesn't need to be able to close its ears, because its ear holes are permanently covered by a thin layer of skin.) Hippopotamuses, which spend much of their time half-submerged in the river, can close their ears, and so can alligators.

Being able to close the ears is a useful ability for animals that live in the water. But they don't use it to block out sounds. We humans can't close our ears at all, but we do have a way of blocking out some of the things we don't want to hear.

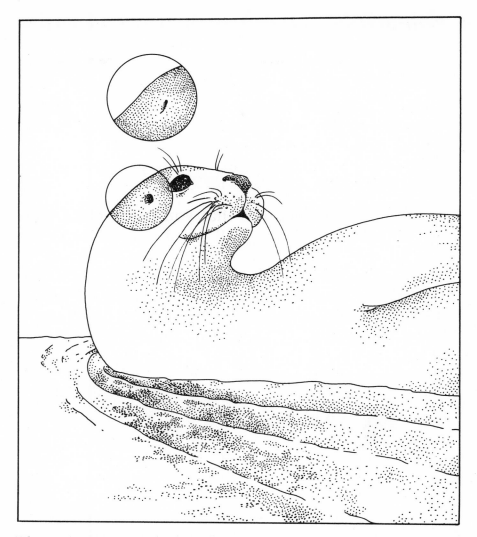

The seal, well adapted for swimming underwater, can close its ears when it dives.

Perhaps you've done it yourself. Have your parents ever complained that you failed to do a chore—and you never heard them asking you to? "What's the matter," they ask, "are you deaf?" Of course not. You can hear the bell of the ice cream truck three blocks away, and you never miss an invitation to a party. You can hear very well—what you *want* to hear.

How is it that you can honestly say you didn't hear your mother ask you to set the table when the sound waves were right there in the air? They traveled down your ear canal, made the eardrum vibrate, were transmitted along the tiny ossicles, went up and down the cochlea, excited all the right hair cells, and sent messages to your brain. Why didn't you hear them?

The answer is in the way the messages from the ears travel through the brain. Before they reach the cerebral cortex, the thinking part of the brain, such messages pass through a region in the center of the brain called the *reticular activating system,* or RAS. "Reticular" means netlike, and this part of the brain is a net of nerve fibers that acts as a sort of clearinghouse. It screens all the messages from the senses and sends on only those that seem interesting, unusual, or important.

Your RAS permits you to "tune out" the traffic noises on a busy street and have a conversation with a friend, even though your friend's voice may actually be quieter than the roaring cars and trucks. You can pick

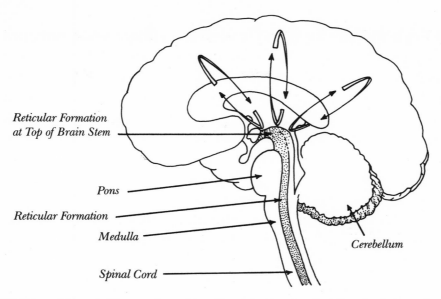

Reticular Formation
at Top of Brain Stem

Pons

Reticular Formation

Medulla

Spinal Cord

Cerebellum

The exchange of messages between the reticular formation and the cerebral cortex

out a single voice when many people are talking. An orchestra conductor can focus his attention on a single violin and pick up any wrong notes it plays, even though a hundred other instruments are playing at the same time.

When you are asleep, the RAS is turned down, but it is still on duty. Only the most important or startling messages are passed on to the cerebral cortex. A parent can sleep peacefully through the rumble of trucks, the wail of sirens, and other night sounds, yet wake instantly if the baby cries.

7 Where Is It? Locating by Sound

In describing the story of your ear, we have generally been talking about just one ear. But of course, you have two. Sounds that reach you are transmitted through both ears, one on each side of your head, and your brain receives messages from both of them. When these two sets of messages are put together, they provide more information than just the pitch, loudness, and quality of the sound. They also give you an idea of where the sound is coming from.

Your ears make a good locating device because they are a head's width apart, and are pointed in different directions. The loudness of a sound decreases with distance. So a sound will seem slightly louder to the ear that is closer to it. That provides one clue. In addition, although sound travels very quickly, it does take time to travel through the air. If a sound is coming from your left, it will reach your left ear a fraction of a second before it reaches your right ear. Your brain can detect a time difference as small as ten milliseconds. (A millisecond is a thousandth of a second.) When you are not sure where a sound is coming from, you may turn your head from side to side to get as much information as possible. Your brain does the computing job automatically, and often so quickly that you are not even aware that you were tracking the source of a sound—you just *know* where it is.

Stereo records use our ability for sound location to "fool" the brain. The sounds produced by part of the orchestra come from one speaker, and part from

That sound must be coming from the left because it reaches the left ear first.

another. When your brain puts together the messages from your right and left ears, it seems as though you are sitting right in the middle of the orchestra. Quadraphonic setups, with the sound divided among four speakers, surround you with sound and produce an even more natural-seeming effect.

Some animals are much better at sound locating than we are. A bat can fly confidently in the dark, snapping up dozens of insects a minute even though it cannot see them. In the laboratory, scientists have had bats fly through a maze of dangling wires that were just barely a wingspan apart. Even wearing a blindfold, a bat can find its way through such a maze without touching a single wire. But if the bat's ears are plugged, or its mouth is taped shut, the bat becomes "blind." It blunders around, bumping into one wire after another. Experiments have shown that bats find their way by sending out bursts of very high frequency sound, about 100,000 cycles per second or even higher. Humans can't hear such high-pitched "ultrasounds," but a bat's ears are more sensitive than ours. The bat's cries bounce off objects in its path, and the sound waves are reflected into its ears. The sound-analyzing areas of a bat's brain are relatively much larger than they are in the human brain. Its brain can put together the sound information to form a picture of dangling wires, or a flying moth, and any other objects around it.

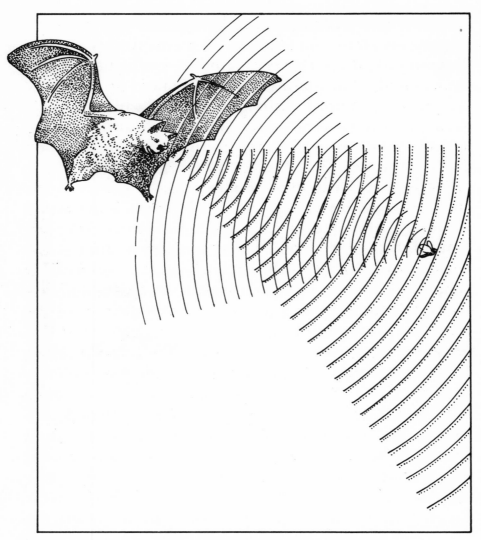

The bat uses bouncing sound waves to locate its prey.

A system of locating objects by sound echoes is called a sonar system. (The radar system used to track the flight paths of airplanes is similar, but it uses radio waves rather than sound waves.) Whales and dolphins also use a form of sonar to find their way around deep in the ocean. It works quite well, for sound is transmitted very effectively through the liquid medium of the ocean water.

People are able to use a sonar system too. Usually we don't develop this ability very much. Our eyes bring us as much information as we need to find our way around. But blind people learn to use their remaining senses more efficiently than most of us do. Often blind people use a variety of sounds, such as hisses, tongue clicks, and the tapping of a cane, to get information about their surroundings. They can learn to tell the size and shape of objects and even to distinguish finer differences, such as between various kinds of cloth. In one experiment, researchers found that blind people could use their own sonar to sense the presence of an object only an inch and three quarters wide at a distance of twenty-four inches, and a ten-inch object nine feet away.

8 The Sense of Balance, or How Your Ears Help You to Ride a Bicycle

Have you ever been seasick? It is a wretched feeling. The world seems to be rocking and swaying under you like a roller coaster. You are dizzy and sick. You may vomit, but even that doesn't help reduce the sick feeling very much. You are pale and cold and sweaty.

Seasickness results from a conflict of sense messages that are being sent to your brain. Your eyes say one thing, but the structures inside your inner ear that normally provide information to keep you right-side-up say something else. The brain tries to make adjustments, but the rocking, swaying motion of the boat or car in which you are riding won't let them work properly.

The inner ear contains two kinds of balance-sensing structures, which provide somewhat different types of information. Both structures are important in keeping you upright, whether you are sitting, standing, walking, running, riding a bike, or spinning around in a pirouette.

The saccule and utricle are called organs of *static* equilibrium. ("Static" means not moving.) They tell you how your head is positioned, relative to the force of gravity. If an airplane pilot's saccule and utricle were damaged, he might come out of a cloud flying upside down. Like the hair cells of the organ of Corti, the cells that line the saccule and utricle are equipped with fine hairs. But these hair cells have small particles of calcium carbonate on their ends. These little particles are called *otoliths,* or "ear stones." If you tip your head, the otoliths move, stimulate the hair cells, and send messages along nerves to the brain.

The three semicircular canals are the organs of dynamic equilibrium. They provide information about movements and changes in position. The three turns of the semicircular canals are arranged at right angles to each other. Two are vertical, and the other is horizontal. They are filled with fluid, and there are hair cells at the base of each canal. Moving your head in any direction will set the fluid in at least one of the semicircular canals moving. The moving fluid excites the hair cells, and they send messages to the brain.

You usually don't have to think about keeping your balance. Your brain processes the messages from the inner ear automatically. If messages from the saccule and utricle say you are tilted, the brain sends its own

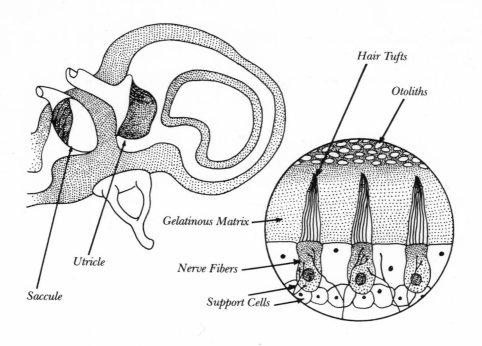

Hair Tufts

Otoliths

Gelatinous Matrix

Nerve Fibers

Support Cells

Utricle

Saccule

messages to the muscles—just the right muscles to get you right side up again. Messages from the semicircular canals are especially helpful. They tell the brain when you are *about* to fall off balance, so the brain can have the muscles make corrections ahead of time, to keep you from falling.

Important information for keeping your balance also comes from some other parts of the body: from the eyes, and from special sense cells in the soles of the feet and the joints of the legs. Spinning around rapidly, as in a merry-go-round, can cause the same

49

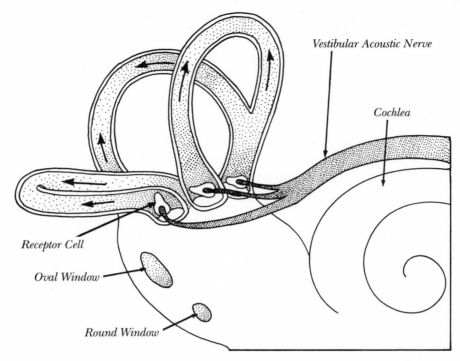

Vestibular Acoustic Nerve

Cochlea

Receptor Cell

Oval Window

Round Window

Arrows indicate ability of fluid within the canals to move when the head is moved.

kinds of problems of conflicting messages as riding in a swaying car or boat. Diseases of the labyrinth can also produce a disturbing dizziness and nausea. There are drugs and surgical treatments that can help in such cases, although many patients get better all by themselves.

9 Too Much Noise!

What is noise? Often the definition depends on who is listening. Your parents may think the latest rock or disco hit is an awful racket, while to you it is just pleasant sound. Circumstances may change the definition, too. Normally you may enjoy listening to music. But when you are doing your homework and trying to work out an especially difficult problem, even a favorite tune may seem like distracting noise.

Usually we reserve the word "noise" for unwanted sounds. Most often they are loud sounds, such as the roar of a vacuum cleaner's motor or a jet plane flying overhead. But soft sounds can be annoying noise, too. The whine of a mosquito near your ear isn't very loud, but it can be upsetting because you know that if the mosquito lands, it may bite you. When you are trying to go to sleep at night, the tick of a clock or the dripping of a leaky faucet, which you normally wouldn't even notice, can become maddening. (In the quiet of the night, with very few other sense messages coming in, your reticular activating system may send on some sound messages to your thinking brain that wouldn't normally get through.)

Some sounds should be considered noise no matter who is listening, and no matter what the circumstances. These are sounds loud enough to damage your hearing. Studies of workers in noisy factories have shown that long periods of working eight hours a day in the presence of noise at a level of 85 decibels or higher produces a gradual loss of hearing. Shorter exposures

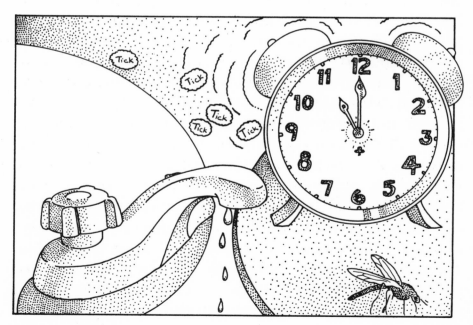

Annoying Noises

to louder noises, such as the amplified music at a rock concert, can have a similar effect. At first the hearing loss is temporary—the hearing comes back to normal after a few hours spent in quiet surroundings. But eventually the damage becomes permanent. Researchers have found that after prolonged exposure to loud noise, such as rock music at 120 decibels, some of the hair cells of the organ of Corti are damaged. These delicate cells cannot be replaced. Once they are destroyed, the ability to hear at those frequencies is permanently lost. When noise produces a loss of hearing, usually the ability to hear high frequencies is lost first, with the lower ones disappearing later.

In our modern world, the amount of noise in our daily lives has been growing each year. Air conditioners, electrical appliances, and power mowers, for example, all contribute to the noise that surrounds us. Traffic noises fill the city streets, and the rumble and whine of trucks on distant highways carries over the countryside. Machinery in factories and offices adds to the clamor.

Even when noises are not loud enough to damage our hearing, they can cause problems. For our long-ago ancestors, loud or sudden noises, from the roar of a lion to the crackling of a twig, were important alarm signals. They alerted the body's systems to prepare for a quick getaway or a stand-up fight. Today, loud and sudden noises are all around us. Our minds know that

they are not important—they don't threaten our lives. But these noises still trigger the same "flight-or-fight" preparations that were so useful to our ancestors long ago. They send messages flashing along our nerves and spark the release of a chemical called *epinephrine,* which is quickly carried through the body by the bloodstream. Both the nerve and the chemical messages act to tense muscles, set the heart beating faster, and produce all the other effects of a typical alarm reaction. The blast of a motorcycle starting up, the hum of an electric blender, the crash of a broken dish has us instantly ready for action. But there's no one to fight, nothing to run away from. It's upsetting.

Studies of factory workers showed that noise above 70 decibels—about the level of sound on a city street—narrowed their arteries and raised their blood pressure. In other studies, noise levels of 90 to 95 decibels (a little less than the sound of a jet plane flying overhead) produced high blood pressure that couldn't be brought back to normal even with drugs. There is even evidence that long exposure to loud noises can cause birth defects.

Loud noises can also wake us up at night, keep us from concentrating, and make us irritable and hard to get along with. Most communities have laws against some forms of noise pollution, but very few do much about enforcing them. The problem of noise pollution has been getting worse. We will have to start doing something about it soon, if we want to save our ears and improve—or even maintain—the quality of our lives.

10 Ears Gone Wrong

A few generations ago, children who were born deaf or lost their hearing at an early age never learned to speak. People referred to them as "deaf-mutes" and thought that they could not be taught to speak. But actually, there is nothing wrong with most deaf people's voices, or with the parts of the brain that work in forming speech. They simply haven't had the experience of hearing speech, and so don't go through the natural process of imitation that people with normal hearing do. With the help of a brave and devoted teacher, Helen Keller, a young girl who was both deaf and blind, showed the world that deaf people *can* be taught to speak and communicate with people around them. Today, there are methods for testing the hearing of very young babies. If there is a hearing problem, doctors try to fit them with a hearing aid before they are a year old, so that they can learn to speak normally.

Damage to any of the links in the chain of hearing, from the eardrum to the brain, can be a cause of deafness. A machine called an audiometer is used to test hearing.

An accident, an infection, or a very loud noise such as a dynamite blast may cause the eardrum to tear or

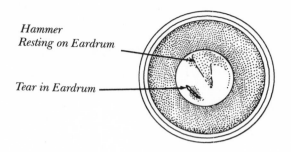

Hammer Resting on Eardrum

Tear in Eardrum

rupture. Small tears in the eardrum usually heal without any permanent damage. But large ones may remain. A ruptured eardrum won't vibrate when sound waves hit it, and so no sound will be transmitted from it. Infections can also cause scarring of the eardrum, which makes it less sensitive. A person with a ruptured eardrum does not lose all the hearing in the ear, since there is some conduction of sound through the bones of the skull as well. Bone conduction explains why your voice sounds different to you than it does when you hear the most faithful tape recording of it. You hear the tape recording through the air, while your own voice comes to you partly through air and partly through the bones of your skull.

Doctors call an inflammation of the middle ear *otitis media.* It can result from an infection or allergy. The membranes swell, and fluid accumulates in the middle ear. A loss of hearing results, but it usually clears up if

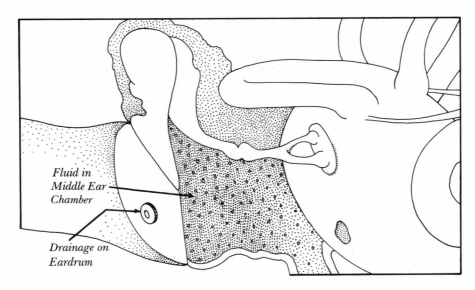

Fluid in Middle Ear Chamber

Drainage on Eardrum

Treatment of otitis media

the inflammation is successfully treated. The doctor may use drugs to shrink the membranes and dry up the extra fluids. A tiny drain may have to be inserted into the eardrum.

Otitis media is common in children. Another type of middle ear deafness is typical of older people. Its medical name is *otosclerosis*. Bony growths form on the tiny bones of the ear, and fuse them together into a single stiff mass, with the footplate of the stirrup firmly anchored to the oval window. When the eardrum vibrates, the bones can't jiggle any longer, so they can't transmit the sound to the inner ear. Surgeons have worked out some effective treatments for this kind of deafness. They may remove the footplate of the stirrup, or replace the entire set of ear bones with an artificial part. Or they may make a new window into the inner ear, covered with a flap of skin.

Various types of hearing aids can also be helpful in treating deafness caused by damage to the sound-conducting systems. Tiny microphones, worn in eyeglass frames or actually inserted into the ear or the skull, can conduct sounds to the inner ear. In an experimental "bionic ear," being developed in Australia, a miniature computer breaks down the electrical signals of a microphone into ten frequencies. Then a bundle of tiny electrodes, implanted inside the ear, stimulates the nerves in the cochlea and sends messages to the brain. With this artificial ear, a deaf person can hear telephones and doorbells ringing and make out words of speech. The quality is not very good yet—like listening to a staticky transmission on international radio. But the researchers hope to improve it.

Inventions like the "bionic ear" may provide hope for people whose deafness is caused by damage to the hair cells in the organ of Corti. Such damage may be produced not only by exposure to loud noises, but also by certain drugs, such as the antibiotic streptomycin. Eventually doctors may also develop ways of helping people who are deaf because of a defect in the last links

in the hearing chain—the nerves and the brain.

The story of your ear is thus a rather complicated one—far more complicated than you may have expected. The ear is a key part of a marvelous hearing system and also an important organ of balance. Ears do not work alone; they are closely linked into a network of nerves and brain centers. With care—which includes avoiding very loud noises whenever possible—a pair of ears can provide a lifetime of service. Medical researchers are steadily gaining new knowledge and techniques to use in keeping ears healthy and repairing them when they go wrong.

Index